al fresco

RYLAND
PETERS
& SMALL
London New York

al fresco

Louise Pickford *photography by* Ian Wallace

First published in Great Britain in 2002
by Ryland Peters & Small
Kirkman House
12–14 Whitfield Street
London W1T 2RP

www.rylandpeters.com

10 9 8 7 6 5 4 3 2 1

Text © Louise Pickford 2002

Design and photographs
© Ryland Peters & Small 2002

Printed in China

ISBN 1 84172 248 0

A CIP record for this book is available
from the British Library.

Senior Designer Steve Painter
Commissioning Editor Elsa Petersen-Schepelern
Production Meryl Silbert
Art Director Gabriella Le Grazie
Publishing Director Alison Starling

Food Stylist Louise Pickford
Props Stylist Heidi Castles
Indexer Hilary Bird

Acknowledgements

The author and publisher would like to thank Keith
& Louise Matheny for allowing us to photograph
aboard their boat M.V. Hattitude in Sydney, and
Les Reedman and Helen Robbins for allowing us
to photograph at their homes. Thanks also to
Cleopatra Blue Mountains, a Relais & Chateaux
property of five guest rooms and restaurant in the
Blue Mountains outside Sydney, NSW, Australia.
Beautiful props were lent to us by Mosmania, of
Mosman, NSW; Bison Homewares, of Deakin in
the Australian Capital Territory (www.bisonhome.
com.au), Room Interior Products of Melbourne and
New York (www.room.com.au) and Lucienne Linen
of Mosman, NSW (www.luciennelinens.com.au).
Our thanks for their assistance.

Notes

All spoon measurements are level unless
otherwise specified.

Ovens should be preheated to the specified
temperature. Recipes in this book were tested
in a fan-assisted oven. If using a regular oven,
increase the oven temperature by 20°C (40°F),
or follow the manufacturer's instructions.

Uncooked or partly cooked eggs should not be
served to the very old or frail, the very young or
to pregnant women.

contents

eating al fresco

Al fresco means 'in the open air' and is synonymous with eating outdoors. Why food tastes better outside is one of life's mysteries. Is it just being in the fresh air on a warm summer's day that is so pleasurable – and eating is merely a way to pass the time – or is there more to it? I definitely think food comes alive in the open air – the colours are more vivid, the smell more evocative and the flavours more satisfying.

Since moving to Australia, I have come to appreciate the true meaning of al fresco eating. Every night during the summer, I see couples snuggled romantically on a bench sipping a glass of wine and sharing a snack, or groups of friends picnicking on a stretch of grass beside the harbour, watching the sunset.

Weekends at the beach are guaranteed to provide the perfect spot for a picnic or barbecue and, in many Australian parks, barbecues are a permanent fixture – you don't even have to worry about bringing your own: you just turn up with the food and coals and start cooking. Some barbecues are even gas-fired: what could be simpler?

I have some great memories of picnics and barbecues in England, where the sometimes inclement weather would have us sheltering under a huge umbrella.

Somehow, it never really seemed to matter: we always had fun and the food still tasted great. Everybody loves eating outside, where we feel happier and healthier. You don't need a glorious view or sandy beach to enjoy it: a table in the garden, on the deck or on a roof terrace still provide us with an opportunity to eat in the fresh air.

It is the food that is important, that takes centre stage. As a food writer, I can think of little that is more exciting than writing recipes that are intended to be eaten al fresco. I hope I have managed to assemble a collection of recipes that will inspire everyone to pack up a lunch and head for the hills – or just onto the balcony.

When planning this book, I tried to think of the kind of food best suited to eating outdoors. Then I realized that was crazy, because all food tastes better in the open air. The result is this collection of my favourite dishes. I have included a range of recipes from the quick and simple for an impromptu picnic, to some that are more involved and which you might like to serve at a special party. There are also some elaborate dishes designed to be eaten within range of the stove for a dinner party in the garden or on the terrace.

Think how you love eating outdoors; lunch in the garden, a barbecue on the beach, a picnic in the country, dinner beside the pool, a packed lunch to take on a hike, food to serve at a drinks party in the garden, brunch on the terrace – the list is endless.

brunch in the sun

Brunch is usually a weekend luxury. It offers us the perfect excuse to linger over breakfast, savouring the fact that we don't have to rush off to work. If it's a sunny morning, that's just the icing on the cake.

Set a tray with your favourite brunch dishes and a large pot of steaming hot coffee or tea. Tuck the newspapers under your arm and head out onto the terrace or deck, or into the garden. Sit in the sun – if that's what you like to do – or snooze in the shade to save your complexion.

Brunch can be marvellous as a solitary indulgence for just yourself and your partner, but it's also a great excuse for casual entertaining. Invite your friends around to share an al fresco meal on a Saturday or Sunday. It sets the scene for a perfect day and, more often than not, brunch turns into a long lunch followed by a relaxing afternoon and, before you know it, early evening drinks – all outdoors. Sounds good enough to eat!

berries with honeyed yoghurt

200 g fresh blueberries

a strip of lemon zest

a squeeze of lemon juice

a pinch of ground cinnamon

600 ml plain yoghurt (not low-fat)

6 tablespoons clear honey

Serves 4–6

Since moving to Sydney, with its wonderful sunny climate, I've discovered the joys of brunch or breakfast eaten outdoors. Breakfast is big in this city, with hundreds of cafés, bistros and bars offering wonderfully light, healthy food to people en route to work. This recipe was inspired by a dish I discovered at one of my favourite places – a café in Balmoral, a pretty beachside suburb.

Reserve a few of the best berries for serving and put the remainder into a saucepan. Add the lemon zest, lemon juice, cinnamon and 1 tablespoon water. Heat gently for about 3 minutes until the berries just start to soften slightly. Let cool.

Spoon the berries into glasses, then add the yoghurt and honey. Top with the reserved berries and serve.

Creamy scrambled eggs topped with rocket pesto are especially good with the extra crunch provided by a nut bread or one made with extra seeds and oat flakes.

12 free range eggs

4 tablespoons double cream

50 g butter

6 slices bread, toasted (preferably walnut bread)

sea salt and freshly ground black pepper

Rocket pesto

50 g rocket

2 tablespoons chopped fresh basil

2 tablespoons blanched almonds, chopped

100 ml extra virgin olive oil

1 garlic clove, chopped

2 tablespoons freshly grated pecorino or Parmesan cheese

sea salt and freshly ground black pepper

Serves 6

creamy eggs
with rocket pesto

To make the rocket pesto, chop the rocket leaves coarsely, then transfer to a food processor. Add the basil, almonds, oil, garlic, salt and pepper and purée briefly to form a vivid green paste. Transfer to a bowl and stir in the freshly grated cheese.

Put the eggs and cream into a bowl, whisk with a fork, then add salt and pepper. Put the butter into a large non-stick saucepan, melt gently, then add the egg mixture and cook, stirring with a wooden fork over a low heat until the eggs have just set.

Put a slice of toast onto each plate, add the scrambled eggs and serve, topped with a spoonful of rocket pesto.

honey-roasted peaches
with ricotta and coffee bean sugar

Grinding whole coffee beans with lump sugar is typically Italian and adds a delicious crunch to the dish. This is a mouthwatering recipe, to be enjoyed on a warm summer morning.

6 large peaches or nectarines

2 tablespoons clear honey

1 tablespoon coffee beans

1 tablespoon lump sugar

300 g chilled ricotta cheese

Serves 6

Cut the peaches or nectarines in half and remove the stones. Line a baking dish with baking parchment and add the peaches or nectarines, cut side up. Drizzle with the honey and roast in a preheated oven at 220°C (425°F) Gas 7 for 15–20 minutes, until the fruit is tender and caramelized. Let cool slightly.

Put the coffee beans and sugar into a coffee grinder and work very briefly, until the beans and sugar are coarsely ground.

Spoon the peaches or nectarines onto plates, top with a scoop of ricotta and a sprinkle of the sugary coffee beans, then serve.

warm blueberry and almond **muffins**

Muffins are quick and easy to prepare and make a lovely breakfast snack, especially when served warm with coffee.

Sift the flour, baking powder and mixed spice into a bowl and stir in the ground almonds and sugar. Put the egg, buttermilk and melted butter into a second bowl and beat well. Stir into the dry ingredients to make a smooth batter.

Fold in the blueberries, then spoon the mixture into 10 of the muffin cases in the muffin tray until three-quarters full. Scatter with the chopped almonds and bake in a preheated oven at 200°C (400°F) Gas 6 for about 18–20 minutes, until risen and golden. Remove from the oven, let cool on a wire rack and serve warm.

200 g plain flour

1 ½ teaspoons baking powder

1 teaspoon ground mixed spice

50 g ground almonds

175 g sugar

1 egg

300 ml buttermilk

50 g butter, melted

250 g blueberries

15 g almonds, chopped

12-hole muffin tin with paper muffin cases

Makes 10

pan bagnat

4 ciabatta rolls

2 garlic cloves, crushed

4 tablespoons extra virgin olive oil

1 tablespoon red wine vinegar

4 ripe tomatoes, thickly sliced

200 g canned tuna in olive oil, drained and flaked

24 pitted black olives, preferably niçoise

12 anchovy fillets in oil, drained

2 tablespoons capers

a few rocket leaves

a handful of basil leaves

sea salt and freshly ground black pepper

Serves 4

Cut the ciabatta rolls in half. Put the garlic, oil and vinegar into a bowl, mix well, then brush all over the cut surfaces of the rolls.

Divide the remaining ingredients between the 4 rolls, add the lids and wrap in clingfilm. Let soak and infuse for at least 1 hour before serving.

warm potato tortilla
with smoked salmon

400 g small, waxy, salad-style potatoes

25 g butter

1 small onion, sliced

4 eggs

250 g smoked salmon

salt and freshly ground black pepper

smoked salmon, salmon caviar (keta) and crème fraîche, to serve

Serves 4

Cook the potatoes in a saucepan of lightly salted, boiling water for 10–12 minutes until cooked but not falling apart. Drain and refresh under cold water. Pat dry and cut into dice.

Put half the butter into a frying pan, melt gently, add the onion and cook gently for 5 minutes. Add the potato slices and cook for a further 5 minutes.

Put the eggs, salt and pepper into a bowl, Whisk well, then stir in the potato and onion mixture. Put the remaining butter into 4 blini pans or 1 frying pan, then add the egg mixture.

Cook over a gentle heat for about 6–8 minutes, then flip the tortilla or transfer to a preheated grill to set and lightly brown the surface. If making a large tortilla, you should cook it for about 10 minutes before grilling.

Let cool a little, then serve topped with smoked salmon, a little salmon caviar and a dollop of crème fraîche.

Traditionally, pan bagnat, from Nice in the South of France, is made in a large baguette, but I prefer to use Italian ciabatta rolls. The tortilla is just one way of serving smoked salmon and eggs for brunch – I like to cook individual tortillas in little blini pans (sold in good cookware stores), but the dish is equally good cooked in a large frying pan and cut into wedges.

salads, soups and starters

Outdoor eating is such a joy in itself that the food needs to be simple – just a few fresh ingredients combined to make both the meal and the experience that little bit better.

Salads, starters and soups can make a whole meal just by themselves. A chilled soup is perfect in summer and a lovely way to start a meal. Remember that a thermos will keep cold soups cold as well as hot ones hot, so what better way to transport it to a picnic. Take along a few big coffee mugs or even paper cups, and soup is the easiest dish in the world to serve. If you're using a thermos, rinse it out with boiling water first if you're using it for hot foods – or with ice cubes and iced water if you're using it for cold foods.

Whatever else you serve outdoors, I think you should serve a salad, too. Sometimes it can be a course in itself sometimes it accompanies other dishes. Keep the leaves rolled up in a cloth in the refrigerator or in a cool box and they'll stay crisp until you serve them.

My favourite starters include the fresh, spicy flavours of East and South-east Asian foods, as well as the strong impact of Italian foods. In fact, I think I prefer these flavours pretty well any time.

summer vegetables
with bagna cauda

Put the bagna cauda – the 'hot bath' – of warm anchovy butter in the centre of the table with a basket of fresh summer vegetables, so everyone can just help themselves.

200 g for each serving of fresh, young, summer vegetables, washed and trimmed, such as baby carrots, baby fennel bulbs, radishes, cherry tomatoes, baby courgettes

Bagna cauda

50 g unsalted butter

3–4 large garlic cloves, crushed

50 g anchovies in oil, drained and chopped

200 ml extra virgin olive oil

Serves 4–6

Arrange the trimmed vegetables in a basket or on a large platter.

To make the bagna cauda, put the butter and garlic into a small saucepan and heat gently. Simmer very slowly for 4–5 minutes until the garlic has softened, but not browned. Add the anchovies, stir well, then pour in the oil. Cook gently for a further 10 minutes, stirring occasionally, until the sauce is soft and almost creamy.

Transfer the sauce to a dish and serve at once with the selection of trimmed vegetables.

summer leaf
and herb **salad**

inner leaves from 2 large cos lettuces

250 g mixed salad leaves, such as radicchio, mâche (lamb's lettuce or corn salad), mizuna or chicory

a handful of mixed, fresh soft-leaf herbs such as basil, chives, dill and mint

Honey lemon dressing

1 garlic clove, crushed

125 ml extra virgin olive oil

1 tablespoon lemon juice

1 teaspoon clear honey

1 teaspoon Dijon mustard

sea salt and freshly ground black pepper

Serves 4

There are thousands of recipes for simple leaf salads, so what makes one better than the next? I think it's just a matter of taste and this version is one of my favourites.

Put the dressing ingredients into a bowl or small jug and set aside to infuse for at least 1 hour. Just before serving, strain out the garlic.

Wash the leaves, spin dry in a salad spinner (or pat dry with kitchen paper) and transfer to a plastic bag. Chill for 30 minutes to make the leaves crisp.

Put the leaves and herbs into a large bowl, add a little of the dressing and toss well to coat evenly. Add a little more dressing to taste, then serve.

broad bean salad
with mint and parmesan

750 g podded, young fresh or frozen broad beans

3 heads of chicory

leaves from 3 sprigs of mint

25 g Parmesan cheese

salt

Hazelnut oil dressing

2 tablespoons extra virgin olive oil

4 tablespoons hazelnut oil*

2 teaspoons white wine vinegar

1 teaspoon Dijon mustard

¼ teaspoon sugar

sea salt and freshly ground black pepper

Serves 6

I like to serve this salad as as part of a tapas spread, but it can be served as a starter or snack, too. If it's early in the season and you have young, tender broad beans, it's not necessary to peel them after blanching. Out of season, you can use frozen broad beans or flat beans cut into 3 cm lengths.

Plunge the broad beans into a saucepan of lightly salted, boiling water, return to the boil and simmer for 1–2 minutes. Drain and refresh the beans immediately under cold running water. Pat dry and peel away the grey-green outer skin if necessary. Put the peeled beans into a salad bowl.

Cut the chicory in half lengthways, slice thickly crossways, then add to the beans. Add the mint leaves, tearing any large ones in half. Using a potato peeler, cut thin shavings of Parmesan over the salad.

Just before serving, put the dressing ingredients into a small jug, mix well, sprinkle over the salad, toss well, then serve.

Note If hazelnut oil is difficult to find, substitute extra virgin olive oil. Always buy nut oils in small quantities and keep them in the refrigerator: they are delicate, and become rancid very quickly.

If you've never eaten a salad in a Japanese restaurant, this will be a delightful surprise. The salad itself is a simple combination of fresh ingredients plus two types of Japanese noodles – but it's the dressing that makes this so interesting.

japanese garden salad with noodles

Cook the noodles separately according to the instructions on the packet. Drain and set aside.

Blanch the mangetout in lightly salted, boiling water for 1 minute. Drain, refresh under cold water and dry well.

Wash and dry the lettuce leaves. Cut the carrot and cucumber into matchsticks and the tomatoes into wedges. Divide the noodles and salad ingredients between 6 serving bowls.

Put the dressing ingredients into a bowl, add 150 ml water and stir well until the sugar has dissolved. Pour over the salad and serve at once.

100 g soba noodles

100 g udon noodles

250 g mangetout

2 cos lettuce hearts or Little Gem lettuces, leaves separated

2 carrots

1 cucumber

4 ripe tomatoes

salt

Japanese dressing

2 tablespoons Japanese soy sauce (shoyu)

1½ tablespoons sugar

1½ tablespoons rice vinegar

1 tablespoon sesame oil

Serves 6

A wonderful and unusual salad that I encountered on a recent trip to Bali. It can be served as part of a savoury spread, as an accompaniment to grilled prawns or even as a pudding.

indonesian chilli
fruit salad

½ ripe pineapple

1 ripe papaya or mango

1 pomelo or pink grapefruit

2 large bananas

2 green apples

Chilli dressing

50 g dark palm sugar
or soft brown sugar,
about 4 tablespoons

4 tablespoons lemon juice

2 tablespoons soy sauce

1–2 red chillies, such as
serrano, deseeded and
finely chopped

Serves 6

To make the dressing, put the sugar, lemon juice, soy sauce and 2 tablespoons water into a small saucepan and heat over a low heat until the sugar has dissolved. Remove from the heat, add the chillies and let cool.

Peel, core and cut the pineapple into wedges, then chunks. Peel, deseed and dice the papaya or mango. Peel the pomelo or grapefruit, cut out the segments, and cut each segment in half. Peel and slice the bananas. Peel, core and dice the apples.

Arrange all the fruits in a large bowl, toss gently in the dressing, then chill for about 15 minutes before serving.

pasta, squash and feta salad
with olive dressing

750 g butternut squash

1 tablespoon extra virgin olive oil

1 tablespoon chopped fresh thyme leaves

500 g dried penne

350 g feta cheese, diced

350 g cherry tomatoes, halved

4 tablespoons chopped fresh basil

4 tablespoons pumpkin seeds, pan-toasted in a dry frying pan

sea salt and freshly ground black pepper

Dressing

150 ml extra virgin olive oil

3 tablespoons tapenade (see recipe introduction)

juice of 1 lemon

1 teaspoon clear honey

sea salt and freshly ground black pepper

Serves 6

Ready made tapenade is available in supermarkets and delicatessens and is usually quite good quality. Some delis make their own and these are definitely worth seeking out for this dish.

Peel and deseed the butternut squash and cut the flesh into bite-sized pieces. Put into a bowl or plastic bag, then add the oil, thyme, salt and pepper, Toss well, then arrange in a single layer in a roasting tin. Roast in a preheated oven at 200°C (400°F) Gas 6 for about 25 minutes until golden and tender. Let cool.

To make the dressing, put the olive oil, tapenade, lemon juice and honey into a bowl. Whisk well, then add salt and pepper to taste.

Bring a large saucepan of lightly salted water to the boil, add the penne and cook for about 10 minutes until *al dente* (just cooked but still slightly crunchy in the middle). Drain well, then immediately stir in 4 tablespoons of the dressing. Let cool.

When cool, put the pasta and squash into a salad bowl, mix gently, then add the feta cheese, cherry tomatoes, basil and toasted pumpkin seeds. Just before serving, stir in the remaining dressing.

chicken salad with radicchio and pine nuts

I love this salad, with its rich, almost plum-like flavours of raisins and Marsala. Sherry vinegar, one of the most delicious vinegars, is sold in larger supermarkets or delicatessens. If you can't find it, use balsamic instead.

1 small red onion, sliced

750 g cooked chicken breast

1 head of radicchio, shredded

125 g rocket leaves

a few sprigs of flat leaf parsley

Marsala raisin dressing

100 ml extra virgin olive oil

50 g pine nuts

75 g raisins

2 tablespoons Marsala wine

2 tablespoons sherry vinegar

sea salt and freshly ground black pepper

Serves 4–6

Put the onion slices into a small bowl and cover with cold water. Let soak for 30 minutes, drain well, then dry thoroughly with kitchen paper.

Tear or slice the chicken into thin strips and put into a large salad bowl. Add the radicchio, rocket leaves, parsley and onion.

To make the dressing, put 2 tablespoons of the oil into a frying pan, heat gently, add the pine nuts and raisins and sauté for 3–4 minutes until the pine nuts are lightly golden. Add the Marsala and vinegar, with salt and pepper to taste, and let warm through. Stir in the remaining oil and remove from the heat.

Pour the dressing over the salad, toss lightly and serve.

fresh oysters with thai dressing

Oysters are an essential outdoor experience, preferably eaten as close to the sea as you can get. Purists would never serve their oysters any way but naked (the oysters, that is), but I like to experiment with different dressings for new taste sensations.

To make the dressing, put the lemongrass, lime leaves, fish sauce, lime juice, mirin and sugar into a blender, then add 2 tablespoons water. Blend well, then set aside to infuse for 2 hours. Strain into a clean bowl and stir in the cucumber and coriander.

Shuck the oysters, reserving as much of their juice as possible. Spoon the dressing over the oysters and serve at once on a bed of ice.

24 fresh oysters
ice cubes, to serve

Thai dressing

1 stalk of lemongrass, very finely sliced

2 kaffir lime leaves, very finely sliced, or the finely grated zest of 1 lime

2 tablespoons Thai fish sauce

1½ tablespoons lime juice

1½ tablespoons mirin (sweetened Japanese rice wine)

1 teaspoon caster sugar

¼ cucumber, peeled and diced

a few coriander leaves

Serves 4

Since moving to Sydney, I have become a real fan of Japanese food, partly for its simplicity, but mainly for its freshness. To make this dish, the tuna you buy must be extremely fresh, so tell your fishmonger that you will be serving the fish raw.

tuna sashimi with pickled ginger dressing

300 g tuna fillet, in the piece
a few salad leaves

Pickled ginger dressing
2 tablespoons Japanese soy sauce (shoyu)
2 tablespoons rice wine vinegar
½ tablespoon sesame oil
½ tablespoon caster sugar
2 tablespoons sliced pickled ginger
1 tablespoon chopped fresh coriander
a little cracked Szechuan pepper or black pepper

Serves 6

Slice the tuna very thinly and arrange on plates.

Put all the dressing ingredients into a bowl or small jug, add 2 tablespoons water and mix well.

Sprinkle over the tuna, top with a few salad leaves and serve at once.

three **salsas**

Salsas give an extra dimension to chicken, meat and fish and are incredibly versatile. The hot pineapple and papaya salsa is good with prawns or pork, the creamy corn salsa marries well with chicken, while the tomato and ginger salsa is very good with white fish or tortilla chips.

creamy corn **salsa**

1 ear of fresh corn,
husk removed

2 red chillies

1 tomato, diced

1 garlic clove, crushed

juice of ½ lime

1 tablespoon maple syrup

2 tablespoons sour cream

sea salt and freshly ground
black pepper

Serves 6

Preheat a barbecue or grill until hot.
Add the corn and cook for about
15 minutes, turning frequently, until
charred on all sides. Let cool.

Add the chillies and grill until the
skins are charred all over. Transfer
to a bowl and cover with a clean
cloth until cool.

Using a sharp knife, cut down
all sides of the corn cob to remove
the kernels. Put them into a bowl.
Peel and deseed the chillies, chop
the flesh and add it to the corn.

Stir in all the remaining ingredients,
season to taste, then serve.

hot pineapple and papaya **salsa**

½ ripe pineapple

½ large papaya

juice of 1 lime

1–2 green chillies, deseeded
and chopped

2 spring onions, finely
chopped

1 tablespoon chopped
fresh mint

1 tablespoon Thai fish sauce

Serves 6

Peel the pineapple, remove and
discard the core, then dice the flesh
and put into a serving bowl,
together with any juice.

Peel the papaya, scoop out the
seeds and dice the flesh. Add to
the pineapple.

Stir in the spring onions, mint and
fish sauce, set aside to infuse for
about 30 minutes, then serve.

tomato, sesame and ginger **salsa**

2 ripe tomatoes, peeled, deseeded
and diced

½ red onion, finely chopped

5 cm fresh ginger, peeled and grated

1 garlic clove, chopped

1 tablespoon chopped fresh coriander

2 tablespoons peanut oil

1 tablespoon soy sauce

1 teaspoon sesame oil

Serves 6

Put all the ingredients into a bowl,
set aside to infuse for about
30 minutes, then serve.

On a hot summer's day, a chilled soup is the perfect lunch dish. Melon with Parma ham is a classic Italian antipasto and is the basis of one of these delicious cold soups. The coconut soup is based on a Thai original – the contrast with the hot, aromatic garlic prawns is just magical.

chilled coconut soup
with sizzling prawns

500 ml coconut milk

300 ml plain yoghurt

1 cucumber, peeled and chopped

2 tablespoons chopped fresh mint

2 tablespoons extra virgin olive oil

2 garlic cloves, thinly sliced

½ teaspoon cumin seeds

a pinch of dried red chilli flakes

8–12 uncooked tiger prawns, peeled and deveined

sea salt and freshly ground black pepper

Serves 4

Put the coconut milk, yoghurt, cucumber and mint into a blender or food processor and blend to a purée. Add salt and pepper to taste. Chill for 1 hour.

Ladle the soup into 4 bowls just before starting to cook the prawns.

Put the oil into a large frying pan and heat gently. Add the garlic, cumin seeds and chilli flakes and fry very gently until the garlic is softened, but not golden. Using a slotted spoon, transfer the garlic to a small plate.

Increase the heat and add the prawns to the pan. Stir-fry for about 3–4 minutes until cooked through. Return the garlic mixture to the pan, stir quickly, then immediately spoon the sizzling hot prawns onto the soup and serve.

chilled melon soup
with serrano ham

4 cantaloupe melons

6 spring onions, finely chopped

2 tablespoons chopped fresh basil

1 tablespoon stem ginger syrup

300 ml plain yoghurt

2 tablespoons dry sherry

2 large slices serrano or Parma ham

sea salt and freshly ground black pepper

ice cubes, to serve

Serves 4

Cut the melons in half and discard the seeds. Scoop out all the flesh and transfer it to a blender. Add the spring onions and basil and blend until smooth.

Add in the ginger syrup, yoghurt and sherry, blend until very smooth and add salt and pepper to taste. Chill for about 1 hour.

Cook the ham under a preheated grill until very crisp and golden. Cool and break into bite-sized pieces.

Pour the soup into chilled bowls or mugs, add a few ice cubes, a sprinkling of crispy ham and a good grinding of black pepper, then serve.

This is just one of those dishes that, once tasted, never forgotten. Pappa al pomodoro is a Tuscan 'soup', although traditionally it is so thick you can almost eat it with a fork! This is my version – slightly more soup-like.

pappa al pomodoro

Put the tomatoes into a saucepan, add the stock, sugar, 2 tablespoons of the oil and the leaves from the oregano and basil. Add a little salt and pepper, then heat slowly to boiling point. Reduce the heat, cover and simmer gently for 30 minutes.

Toast the bread on a preheated medium-hot barbecue or a stove-top grill pan until charred. Rub the bread all over with the garlic, then transfer to a plate. Sprinkle with the remaining oil and, using a fork, mash well into the bread, breaking it into small bits.

Add the bread to the soup and stir over a low heat for about 5 minutes until the bread has been evenly incorporated and the soup thickened.

Add salt and freshly ground black pepper to taste and serve hot, topped with a little grated Parmesan. This dish is also delicious served cold.

1 kg ripe red tomatoes, preferably on the vine, chopped

300 ml vegetable stock

1 teaspoon caster sugar

6 tablespoon extra virgin olive oil

4 sprigs of oregano

4 sprigs of basil

125 g day-old bread, without crusts

2 garlic cloves

sea salt and freshly ground black pepper

freshly grated Parmesan cheese, to serve

Serves 4

vegetables and vegetarian

Summer is prime vegetable growing season, so it's no wonder this is the time when we can indulge ourselves in the ripest, reddest tomatoes, the crispest shoots of asparagus, the juiciest leaves of salads and herbs. Pick them in their prime (if you're lucky enough to have your own garden) or shop at a greengrocer who takes pride in the quality of his produce – then you can be sure of the finest flavour and quality.

You don't have to be a vegetarian to appreciate wonderful vegetable dishes. In fact, even if you're doing a serious meat-lover's barbecue, you'll need lots of delicious vegetable accompaniments to serve with the main course. I love to cook vegetables on the barbecue, then serve them on a large platter with a large bowl of unctuous mayonnaise for dipping, so everyone can help themselves.

They're equally good turned into a main course in their own right: think of vegetable-based tarts and quiches, or pita breads and picnic loaves stuffed with vegetables and sauces such as pesto. Vegetable pasta, frittata and risotto are all substantial enough to become the main event for lunch in the garden on a summer's day.

grilled corn
with chilli salt rub

One of the America's most popular chillies is the ancho, the dried version of the poblano. When ground to a fine powder, it has a smoky flavour and is mild to medium on the heat scale – delicious with the sweet, nutty taste of corn.

6 ears of corn,
husks removed

2 tablespoons extra virgin
olive oil, plus extra to serve

3 ancho chillies

1½ tablespoons sea salt

3 limes, cut into wedges

Serves 6

Trim the ends of the corn. Bring a large saucepan of lightly salted water to the boil, add the corn and boil for 5 minutes. Drain and refresh under cold water. Pat dry.

Preheat a barbecue or grill until hot. Brush the corn with oil and cook on the barbecue or under the grill for 6–8 minutes, turning frequently until charred all over.

Meanwhile, remove the stalk and seeds from the dried chillies. Chop the flesh coarsely and, using a spice grinder or mortar and pestle, grind to a powder. Transfer to a small bowl, then mix in the salt.

Rub the lime wedges vigorously over the corn, sprinkle with the chilli salt and serve with extra oil for drizzling.

barbecued artichokes
with chilli lime mayonnaise

Try to find small or baby artichokes for this dish so that they can be cooked straight on the barbecue without any blanching first.

18 small artichokes

1 lemon, halved

2 tablespoons extra virgin olive oil

sea salt and freshly ground black pepper

lime wedges, to serve

Chilli lime mayonnaise

1 dried chipotle chilli

2 egg yolks

300 ml olive oil

juice of 1 lime

sea salt

Serves 6

To make the mayonnaise, cover the dried chilli with boiling water and let soak for 30 minutes. Drain and pat dry, then cut in half and scrape out the seeds.

Finely chop the flesh and put into a food processor. Add the egg yolks and a little salt and blend briefly until frothy. With the blade running, drizzle the oil through the funnel until the sauce is thick and glossy. Add the lime juice and, if the mayonnaise is too thick, a tablespoon of warm water. Taste and adjust the seasoning, then cover and set aside.

Trim the stalks from the artichokes and cut off the top 2 cm of the globes. Slice the globes in half lengthways, cutting out the central 'choke' if necessary. Rub the cut surfaces all over with lemon juice to stop them discolouring.

Toss the artichokes with the oil and a little salt and pepper. Cook over medium-hot coals for 15–20 minutes, depending on size, until charred and tender, turning halfway through the cooking time. Serve with the mayonnaise and wedges of lime.

slow-roasted tomatoes
with ricotta and spaghetti

A pasta dish packed full of the flavours of the Mediterranean – garlic, tomatoes, oregano and ricotta. Roast the tomatoes ahead of time if you like and then reheat at 180°C (350°F) Gas 4 for 15 minutes.

6 large, ripe tomatoes

4 sprigs of oregano, plus 2 tablespoons chopped fresh oregano

7 tablespoons extra virgin olive oil

500 g spaghetti

4 garlic cloves, sliced

1 dried red chilli, chopped

juice of ½ lemon

200 g fresh ricotta cheese, crumbled into big pieces

sea salt and freshly ground black pepper

freshly grated Parmesan, to serve

Serves 4

Cut the tomatoes in half and arrange, cut side up, in a shallow roasting tin. Sprinkle with the sprigs of oregano, 1 tablespoon of the oil and lots of salt and pepper.

Roast in a preheated oven at 250°C (500°F) Gas 9 for 20 minutes. Reduce to 150°C (300°F) Gas 2 and cook for a further 1–1½ hours until the tomatoes are golden, glossy and reduced in size by about one-third. Remove from the oven and keep them warm.

Bring a large saucepan of lightly salted water to the boil, add the spaghetti, then return to the boil and cook for about 10 minutes until the pasta is *al dente* (just cooked, but still slightly crunchy in the middle).

After about 5 minutes, put the remaining oil into a large, deep frying pan, heat well, add the garlic and fry gently for 2 minutes until softened but not golden. Add the chilli and cook for a further minute.

Drain the cooked pasta, reserving 4 tablespoons of the cooking liquid. Add the pasta and the reserved cooking liquid to the frying pan, then add the chopped oregano, lemon juice and salt and pepper. Toss over the heat for about 2 minutes.

Transfer to plates and serve topped with the tomatoes and ricotta and a light dusting of grated Parmesan.

50 g butter

1 large onion, finely chopped

2 garlic cloves, crushed

1 leek, trimmed and sliced

300 g arborio rice

150 ml dry vermouth or fino sherry

1 litre vegetable stock

350 g fresh or frozen peas

125 g cos lettuce leaves, washed and shredded

4 tablespoons chopped fresh mint, plus extra mint leaves, to serve

50 g mascarpone cheese

75 g freshly grated Parmesan cheese

sea salt and freshly ground black pepper

Serves 4–6

Although this risotto is best made with fresh peas, you can also use frozen. The mint adds a delicious fresh flavour. This will serve four as a main course or six as a starter.

fresh pea and lettuce **risotto**

Put the butter into a saucepan, melt gently, then add the onion, garlic and leek and fry gently for 10 minutes until softened but not golden. Add the rice, stir for 1 minute until all the grains are glossy, then add the vermouth or sherry. Let bubble and evaporate.

Meanwhile, put the stock into a separate saucepan and heat until just barely simmering. Add about 150 ml of the vegetable stock to the rice. Add the peas and a little salt and pepper, then stir until the liquid has been absorbed. Continue adding the stock and stirring the rice until almost all the stock has been used. Add the lettuce, chopped mint and the remaining stock and cook until absorbed.

Remove from the heat, stir in the mascarpone and 25 g of the Parmesan and season to taste. Cover the pan and set aside for 5 minutes before serving, topped with the remaining Parmesan and mint leaves.

With its lovely, earthy flavours, a frittata is an Italian version of the Spanish tortilla or the French omelette and different ingredients are added depending on the region or season.

mixed mushroom **frittata**

3 tablespoons extra virgin olive oil

2 shallots, finely chopped

2 garlic cloves, finely chopped

1 tablespoon chopped fresh thyme leaves

300 g mixed wild and cultivated mushrooms, such as girolle, chanterelle, portobello, shiitake and cep

6 eggs

2 tablespoons chopped, fresh flat leaf parsley

sea salt and freshly ground black pepper

Serves 6

Put 2 tablespoons of the oil into a non-stick frying pan, heat gently, then add the shallots, garlic and thyme. Fry gently for 5 minutes until softened but not browned.

Meanwhile, brush off any dirt clinging to the mushrooms and wipe the caps. Chop or slice coarsely and add to the pan. Fry for 4–5 minutes until just starting to release their juices. Remove from the heat.

Put the eggs into a bowl with the parsley and a little salt and pepper, whisk briefly, then stir in the mushroom mixture. Wipe the frying pan clean.

Heat the remaining tablespoon of oil in the clean pan and pour in the egg and mushroom mixture. Cook over medium heat for 8–10 minutes until set on the bottom. Transfer to a preheated grill and cook for about 2–3 minutes until the top is set and spotted brown. Cool and serve at room temperature.

roquefort and walnut tart

Blue cheese imparts a wonderful richness of flavour to this light creamy tart with walnut pastry. I like to serve it as a starter with a salad made from rocket, pears and walnuts.

To make the pastry, put the walnuts into a dry frying pan and cook for 1–2 minutes until they start to smell toasted. Transfer to a bowl and let cool. When cool, transfer to a food processor or blender and grind to a meal. Sift the flour and salt into a bowl and rub in the butter until the mixture resembles fine breadcrumbs. Stir in the ground walnuts and then enough cold water to form a soft dough, about 1–2 tablespoons. Transfer the dough to a lightly floured surface, knead gently, then shape into a flat disc. Wrap in clingfilm and chill for about 30 minutes.

Transfer the dough to a lightly floured surface, roll out to a disc about 25 cm in diameter and use to line the flan tin. Prick the base with a fork and chill for a further 30 minutes. Remove from the refrigerator and line the pastry case with baking parchment and baking beans or rice. Bake in a preheated oven at 200°C (400°F) Gas 6 for 10 minutes. Remove the paper and beans or rice and bake for a further 5–6 minutes until the pastry is crisp and lightly golden. Remove from the oven and let cool for about 10 minutes.

Meanwhile, to prepare the filling, dice the Roquefort and put into a food processor. Add the ricotta, cream, eggs, walnut oil, salt and pepper and blend briefly until mixed but not smooth. Pour into the pastry case and cook for about 20 minutes until risen and golden. Let cool slightly in the tin, then serve warm.

To make the salad, put the walnuts into a dry frying pan and toast until golden. Remove, cool and chop coarsely. Peel, core and slice the pears and put into a bowl. Add the rocket, parsley and walnuts.

Put the walnut oil into a measuring cup, add the olive oil, sherry vinegar, honey, salt and pepper and whisk well. Pour over the salad, toss gently, then serve with the tart.

15 g walnuts
100 g plain flour
1 teaspoon salt
50 g butter, diced

Roquefort filling
100 g Roquefort cheese
200 g ricotta cheese
150 ml double cream
3 eggs, lightly beaten
2 tablespoons walnut oil
salt and pepper

Rocket Salad
2 ripe pears
200 g rocket
a handful of parsley
50 g walnuts
4 tablespoons walnut oil
2 tablespoons olive oil
2 teaspoons sherry vinegar
1 teaspoon clear honey
salt and pepper

23 cm flan tin, buttered
baking parchment
baking beans or raw rice

Serves 6

What is it about caramelized onions? They smell just divine, especially when cooked in butter. These simple onion tarts, topped with creamy goats' cheese, are best served warm, although they are also good cold.

onion, thyme and goats' cheese **tarts**

40 g butter

500 g onions, finely sliced

2 garlic cloves, crushed

1 tablespoon chopped fresh thyme leaves

350 g ready-made puff pastry, defrosted if frozen

flour, for rolling out

200 g log goats' cheese

sea salt and freshly ground black pepper

Makes 8

Put the butter into a frying pan, let melt over low heat, then add the onion, garlic and thyme and fry gently for 20–25 minutes, until softened and golden. Let cool.

Put the pastry onto a lightly floured surface and roll out to form a rectangle, 20 x 40 cm, trimming the edges. Cut the rectangle in half lengthways and into 4 crossways, making 8 pieces, about 10 cm square.

Divide the onion mixture between the squares, spreading it over the top, leaving a thin border around the edges. Cut the cheese into 8 slices and arrange in the centre of each square.

Transfer the pastries to a large baking tray and bake in a preheated oven at 220°C (425°F) Gas 7 for about 12–15 minutes until the pastry has risen and the cheese is golden. Let cool a little, then serve warm.

turkish **pizza turnover**

This is similar to the Italian 'calzone' or stuffed pizza. I first came across it in Sydney at a local food market. At one stall, Turkish chefs were busily kneading, rolling and cooking these quite delicious pizzas, which were then cut into strips and served on napkins.

Sift the flour into the bowl of an electric mixer* with dough hook attached. Stir in the yeast and salt. Add the oil and 150–175 ml warm water and work to a dough. Transfer to a floured surface and knead for 10 minutes until the dough is smooth and elastic.

Meanwhile, to make the filling, discard any thick spinach stalks, then wash the leaves in a colander. Drain, transfer to a large saucepan and heat gently for 2–3 minutes until the leaves have wilted. Rinse under cold water, drain completely and squeeze out as much water as possible. Finely chop the spinach and set aside.

Heat the oil in a frying pan, add the onion and garlic and fry gently for 5 minutes until very soft and lightly golden. Stir in the spinach, the 2 cheeses, nutmeg and pepper, then remove from the heat.

Transfer the dough back onto a floured surface and knead it gently. Divide the dough into 4 equal pieces and roll out each piece to a rectangle 20 x 40 cm (it will be very thin). Spread a quarter of the spinach mixture over half the dough, fold over and seal the edges. Repeat with the other pieces of dough to make 4 turnovers.

Heat the flat plate of a barbecue for 5 minutes, then reduce the heat to medium. Brush with a little oil, add the stuffed pizzas and cook for about 4–5 minutes on each side until golden. Alternatively, if you don't have a barbecue, cook on a flat griddle or large, heavy-based frying pan. Serve hot.

*Note If you don't have an electric mixer, use a food processor with the plastic blade attachment, or make by hand in a large mixing bowl. Gradually work the mixture together with your hands to form a soft dough, then turn out onto a lightly floured surface and knead for 8–10 minutes until the dough becomes smooth and elastic.

350 g strong white flour, plus extra for kneading

1½ teaspoons easy-blend dried yeast

1½ teaspoons sea salt

1 tablespoon extra virgin olive oil

Cheese and spinach filling

500 g spinach leaves

1 tablespoon extra virgin olive oil

1 small onion, finely chopped

2 garlic cloves, crushed

125 g feta cheese, crumbled

2 tablespoons grated Parmesan cheese

2 tablespoons mascarpone cheese

a little grated nutmeg

freshly ground black pepper

Serves 4

beetroot hoummus
with pan-grilled bread

Beetroot hoummus is a delicious summery dip for vegetables or toasted bread. Cooking bread on the barbecue or a ridged stove-top grill pan is easy and very like the traditional way that pita bread is cooked.

250 g cooked beetroot in natural juices, drained and chopped

25 g white breadcrumbs

1 garlic clove, crushed

3 tablespoons extra virgin olive oil

2 tablespoons hot horseradish sauce

1 tablespoon freshly squeezed lemon juice

sea salt and freshly ground black pepper

Bread

250 g strong white flour, plus extra for kneading

1 teaspoon sea salt

1 teaspoon easy-blend dried yeast

1 tablespoon olive oil, plus extra for oiling the bowl

Serves 6

To make the bread dough, sift the flour into the bowl of an electric mixer* with the dough hook attached. Stir in the salt and yeast, then gradually work in 125 ml warm water and the oil to make a soft dough. Transfer to a lightly floured surface and knead for about 8–10 minutes until smooth and elastic.

Put the dough into an oiled bowl, cover with clingfilm and let rise in a warm place for 45 minutes or until doubled in size.

Meanwhile, to make the hoummus, put the beetroot, breadcrumbs, oil, horseradish and lemon juice into a food processor, blend to a smooth purée and season with salt and pepper to taste.

Transfer the dough to a lightly floured surface and knead it gently. Divide into 6 pieces and roll out each one to an oval, about the size of a pita bread. Cook the bread over medium-hot coals or on a ridged stove-top grill pan for 1–2 minutes on each side. Serve warm with the hoummus.

*Note If you don't have an electric mixer, use a food processor with the plastic blade attachment, or make by hand in a large mixing bowl. Gradually work the mixture together with your hands to form a soft dough, then invert onto a lightly floured surface and knead for 8–10 minutes until the dough becomes smooth and elastic.

focaccia topped with cherry tomatoes and pesto

The secret to making focaccia is to let the dough rise three times rather than twice, as for regular bread dough. It is well worth the extra 30 minutes needed, as the result is light, airy and totally moreish!

15 g fresh yeast or
½ tablespoon easy-blend
dried yeast

a pinch of sugar

350 g plain white flour,
plus extra for kneading

1 tablespoon sea salt, plus
extra for cooking

2 tablespoons extra virgin
olive oil, plus extra for
drizzling

175 g cherry tomatoes,
halved

40 g pitted black olives,
halved

Pesto

25 g basil leaves

1 garlic clove, crushed

2 tablespoons pine nuts

6 tablespoons extra virgin
olive oil

2 tablespoons freshly grated
Parmesan cheese

sea salt and freshly ground
black pepper

a baking tin, 20 x 30 cm

Serves 8

Put the yeast into a small bowl, add the sugar and 225 ml warm water and stir until the yeast has dissolved. Add 2 tablespoons of the flour and leave in a warm place for 10 minutes until frothy.

Sift the remaining flour and the 1 tablespoon salt into the bowl of an electric mixer fitted with a dough hook and add the frothed yeast mixture and oil. Mix for 10 minutes until smooth and elastic. Shape into a ball, transfer to an oiled bowl, cover with clingfilm and let rise for 1 hour or until doubled in size.

Transfer the dough to a lightly floured surface, knead gently, then shape or roll into a rectangle to fit snugly into the baking tin. Cover and let rise for 30 minutes.

Using your fingers, press indentations all over the surface of the dough. Cover again and let rise for a further 1 hour until well risen.

Meanwhile, to make the pesto, put the basil leaves, garlic, pine nuts and olive oil into a food processor and purée to form a vivid green paste. Transfer to a bowl and stir in the cheese and salt and pepper to taste.

Spread 2–3 tablespoons of the pesto* carefully over the risen dough without letting it collapse. Add the tomatoes and olives and sprinkle with a little more oil and about ½ tablespoon sea salt. Bake in a preheated oven at 200°C (400°F) Gas 6 for about 25 minutes until risen and golden. Cool on a wire rack and serve warm.

***Note** Store the remaining pesto in an airtight container in the refrigerator for up to 3 days and use as a pasta sauce or in the stuffed picnic loaf, page 80.

stuffed **picnic loaf**

Great for a picnic – a loaf packed with barbecued vegetables, pesto and goats' cheese. Make it a day ahead so it can be 'pressed' overnight in the refrigerator for the flavours to develop and mingle.

1 round loaf of bread, about 23 cm diameter, 10 cm high

2 tablespoons extra virgin olive oil

½ quantity pesto (page 67)

2 large red onions

2 large red peppers

2 large courgettes

250 g soft goats' cheese, diced

12 large basil leaves

sea salt and freshly ground black pepper

Serves 6

Cut the top off the loaf and carefully scoop out most of the bread, leaving just the outer shell (reserve the bread and make into crumbs for another dish). Put 1 tablespoon of the oil into a bowl, stir in the pesto and spread half the mixture around the inside of the shell and lid. Set aside.

Cut the onions into wedges, brush with a little of the remaining tablespoon of oil and cook on a preheated barbecue or on a stove-top grill pan for 10 minutes on each side until very tender. Let cool.

Char-grill the peppers on a preheated barbecue or stove-top grill pan or under an overhead grill for about 15 minutes until blackened all over. Transfer to a plastic bag and let cool. Peel away the skin, discard the seeds and cut the flesh into quarters, reserving any juices.

Cut the courgettes lengthways into 2 mm thick slices, brush with oil and barbecue or grill as above for 2–3 minutes on each side until lightly charred and softened. Let cool.

Arrange the filling in layers inside the loaf, with the goats' cheese and remaining pesto in the middle. Sprinkle with any remaining oil and the pepper juices and replace the lid.

Wrap the whole loaf in clingfilm and put onto a plate. Top with a board and a heavy food can to weigh it down. Chill in the refrigerator overnight.

The next day, cut into wedges and serve.

fish and seafood

My favourite holiday memories are of walking along a beach or harbour and being seduced by the aromas issuing from nearby tavernas or cafés – the smell of calamari or prawns being grilled over charcoal to be served simply dressed with a drizzle of local olive oil and a squeeze of lemon.

Cooking such delights for yourself is very easy and very rewarding – and if you happen to be near the sea, that's even better. If you normally shy away from cooking fish and seafood indoors, then barbecuing outdoors is the solution. Most of the recipes in this chapter can just as easily be cooked on a barbecue as in a pan or in the oven, and those that do require a stove are ideal for when you entertain in the garden.

Remember, summer is the time when light, healthful fish and seafood are particularly appealing. Fish markets and supermarkets see this as their prime season, so you'll find the best and freshest ingredients on sale. Prawns and lobsters, crabs and squid, clams and mussels, wild fish and farmed – take your pick and give your guests a treat.

tiger prawns with herb mayonnaise

1 kg cooked tiger prawns

lemon wedges, to serve

Herb mayonnaise

2 egg yolks

1 tablespoon lemon juice

1 teaspoon Dijon mustard

300 ml olive oil

4 tablespoons chopped mixed herbs, such as basil, chives, chervil, dill, parsley and tarragon

sea salt and freshly ground black pepper

Serves 6

Summer and picnics are all about this type of simple, delicious, messy food. Peel big, juicy, cooked prawns, then dunk them into a bowl of wonderful homemade herb mayonnaise. Use a plain olive oil, rather than extra virgin for mayonnaise, or it can be rather bitter.

To make the mayonnaise, put the egg yolks, lemon juice, mustard and a little salt and pepper into a food processor and blend briefly until frothy. With the motor running, slowly pour the oil through the funnel to make a thick, glossy sauce. If it becomes too thick, thin it with a little warm water. Add the chopped herbs and blend again until the mayonnaise is a vibrant speckled green.

Peel the prawns and serve with the mayonnaise and wedges of lemon.

Meat and fish (the old-fashioned surf 'n' turf)
can work well and this recipe is a perfect
example of this balance of strong flavours.
I use the chorizo sausage that needs cooking,
rather than the cured tapas variety, although
either would do.

prawn, chorizo and sage **skewers**

300 g uncooked chorizo
24 large, uncooked, peeled prawns, deveined
24 large sage leaves
extra virgin olive oil
lemon juice
freshly ground black pepper

12 skewers, metal or bamboo (if using bamboo,
soak them in warm water for 30 minutes)

Serves 6

Cut the chorizo into 24 slices about 1 cm thick and
thread onto the skewers, alternating with the prawns
and sage leaves. Put a little oil and lemon juice into
a small bowl or jug, mix well, then drizzle over the
skewers. Sprinkle with pepper.

Meanwhile, preheat an overhead grill, stove-top grill
pan or barbecue until hot. Cook the skewers for
1½–2 minutes on each side until the chorizo and
prawns are cooked through. Serve at once.

I've always been a fan of coconut since I first fell in love with my mother's coconut pyramid biscuits! These days, I'm more fascinated with the combinations found in Indonesian and Thai cooking. Seafood has a natural affinity with coconut and you'll love this combination.

lemongrass skewered scallops
with coconut dressing

24 large king scallops, without corals

2 tablespoons peanut oil

grated zest of 2 limes

2 red chillies, deseeded and chopped

2 teaspoons grated fresh ginger

1 garlic clove, crushed

1 tablespoons Thai fish sauce

Coconut milk dressing

125 ml coconut milk

1 tablespoon Thai fish sauce

2 teaspoons caster sugar

2 teaspoons coconut or rice wine vinegar*

6 bamboo skewers, soaked in warm water for 30 minutes

Serves 6

Trim the tough white muscle from the side of each scallop. Put the scallops into a shallow non-metal dish.

Put the peanut oil, lime zest, chillies, ginger, garlic and fish sauce into a small jug or bowl, mix well, then pour over the scallops. Let marinate in the refrigerator for 1 hour.

To make the dressing, put the coconut milk, fish sauce, sugar and vinegar into a small saucepan, heat gently to dissolve the sugar, then bring to a gentle simmer until thickened slightly. Remove from the heat and let cool completely.

Meanwhile, preheat an overhead grill, stove-top grill pan or barbecue until hot.

Thread the scallops onto the prepared skewers and cook for 1 minute on each side. Don't overcook or the scallops will be tough. Serve with the coconut dressing.

*Note Coconut or palm vinegar are used in Thailand and the Philippines: both are milder than regular vinegars. Buy them in Asian food stores or use white rice vinegar as an alternative.

squid piri-piri

Piri-piri, a Portuguese chilli condiment traditionally used to baste grilled chicken, is a combination of chopped red chillies, olive oil and vinegar. It is generally very hot and only a drizzle is needed to add spice to grilled food. Here I have tempered the heat, but you can use more chillies if you like it hotter. It works very well with squid.

8 medium squid tubes, about 250 g each*

freshly squeezed juice of 1 lemon, plus extra lemon wedges, to serve

sea salt

Piri-piri sauce

8 small red chillies

300 ml extra virgin olive oil

1 tablespoon white wine vinegar

sea salt and freshly ground black pepper

16 bamboo skewers, soaked in warm water for 30 minutes

Serves 4

To prepare the squid, put the squid tube on a board and, using a sharp knife, cut down one side and open the tube out flat. Scrape away any remaining insides and wash and dry well.

Skewer each opened-out tube with 2 skewers, running them up the long sides of each piece. Rub a little sea salt over each one and squeeze over the lemon juice. Marinate in the refrigerator for 30 minutes.

Meanwhile, to make the piri-piri, finely chop the whole chillies without deseeding them and transfer to a small jar or bottle. Add the oil, vinegar and a little salt and pepper. Shake well and set aside.

Meanwhile, preheat an overhead grill, stove-top grill pan or barbecue until hot.

Baste the squid with a little of the piri-piri and cook for 1–1½ minutes on each side until charred. Drizzle with extra sauce and serve with lemon wedges.

***Note** If the squid includes the tentacles, cut them off in one piece, thread with a skewer and cook and marinate in the same way as the tubes.

grilled lobsters with 'burnt' butter

I use just the lobster tails for this recipe. If your lobsters have claws, remember to crack them before serving. You can also cook this recipe with either langoustines or large tiger prawns.

6 uncooked lobster tails
or 12 large langoustines
or prawns*

2 tablespoons olive oil

125 g butter

sea salt and freshly ground
black pepper

To serve

lemon wedges

green salad

Serves 6

Using a very sharp knife, cut the lobster tails in half lengthways, cutting down through the shell. Brush the flesh with oil and season well with salt and pepper.

Preheat a stove-top grill pan or barbecue until medium hot. Add the lobster tails and cook, shell side down, for about 5 minutes. Brush with more oil and cook, flesh side down, for a further 3 minutes. Remove from the heat and let rest for 5 minutes.

Put the butter into a small saucepan and heat gently until melted and golden. Arrange the lobster tails on a large platter, drizzle with the butter and squeeze the lemon wedges over the top. Serve with a little green salad.

*Note If using langoustines or prawns, simply cut them in half and discard the vein running along the back of each one. Cook as above for 2 minutes each side until cooked through.

grilled **miso cod**

This marinade is typical of Japanese cooking and imparts a really fantastic flavour to the fish. Miso is a fermented soybean-based paste, available in Asian stores and some larger supermarkets and food stores. As a guide, the lighter the colour, the sweeter the flavour.

3 tablespoons Japanese soy sauce (shoyu)

3 tablespoons sake

3 tablespoons clear honey

2 tablespoons miso paste

6 cod fillets, 200 g each

vegetable oil, for brushing

To serve

pickled ginger

stir-fried baby bok choy

steamed rice

Serves 6

Put the soy sauce, sake, honey and miso into a small saucepan and heat gently until smooth. Set aside to cool completely. Pour into a shallow dish, add the cod fillets, cover and let marinate in the refrigerator for at least 4 hours.

Return to room temperature for 1 hour before cooking. Transfer the fillets to a foil-lined grill pan and cook under a preheated grill for 4 minutes on each side, basting halfway through. Let rest for 5 minutes, then serve with pickled ginger, stir-fried bok choy and rice.

barbecued fish bathed in oregano and lemon

I have many fond memories of summer holidays in Greece – and none is more prized than the smell of seafood emanating from the dozens of little tavernas dotted along the beach. This is a typical dish of char-grilled bream with oil, oregano and garlic, but you could use other small fish such as red mullet, snapper or even trout.

2 lemons

250 ml extra virgin olive oil

1 tablespoon dried oregano

2 garlic cloves,
finely chopped

2 tablespoons chopped
fresh flat leaf parsley

6 snapper or bream, about
350 g each, well cleaned
and scaled

sea salt and freshly ground
black pepper

Serves 6

Grate the zest of 1 lemon into a small bowl and squeeze in the juice. Add 225 ml of the oil, the oregano, garlic, parsley, salt and pepper. Leave to infuse for at least 1 hour.

Wash and dry the fish inside and out. Using a sharp knife, cut several slashes into each side. Squeeze the juice from the remaining lemon into a bowl, add the remaining 4 tablespoons of oil, salt and pepper and rub the mixture all over the fish.

Heat the flat plate of your barbecue for 10 minutes, add the fish and cook for 3–4 minutes on each side until charred and cooked through. Alternatively, use a large, heavy-based frying pan or stove-top grill pan. Transfer to a large, warm platter, pour over the dressing and let rest for 5 minutes before serving.

A great way to prepare whole salmon is to remove the central bone from the fish, then tie the two fillets back together. If your filleting skills are limited, just ask your friendly fishmonger to fillet the whole fish for you.

whole salmon stuffed with herbs

Put the salmon fillets flat onto a board, flesh side up. Carefully pull out any remaining bones with tweezers.

Put the butter, herbs, lemon zest, garlic and plenty of pepper into a small bowl and beat well. Spread the mixture over one of the salmon fillets and put the second on the top, arranging them top to tail.

Using kitchen string, tie the fish together at 2.5 cm intervals. Brush with a little oil, sprinkle with salt and freshly ground black pepper and cook on the flat plate of a barbecue for 10 minutes on each side. Let rest for a further 10 minutes. Remove the string and serve the fish cut into portions.

2 kg whole salmon, filleted

125 g butter, softened

25 g chopped, fresh soft-leaf mixed herbs, such as basil, chives, mint, parsley and tarragon

grated zest of 1 lemon

1 garlic clove, crushed

sea salt and freshly ground black pepper

olive oil, for brushing

Serves 8

peppered tuna steak
with salsa rossa

Salsa rossa is one of those divine Italian sauces that transforms simple meat and fish dishes into food nirvana. The slight sweetness from the peppers is a good foil for the spicy pepper crust.

6 tablespoons mixed peppercorns, coarsely crushed

6 tuna steaks, 200 g each

1 tablespoon extra virgin olive oil

salad leaves, to serve

Salsa rossa

1 large red pepper

1 tablespoon extra virgin olive oil

2 garlic cloves, crushed

2 large ripe tomatoes, peeled and roughly chopped

a small pinch of dried chilli flakes

1 tablespoon dried oregano

1 tablespoon red wine vinegar

sea salt and freshly ground black pepper

Serves 6

To make the salsa rossa, grill the pepper until charred all over, then put into a plastic bag and let cool. Remove and discard the skin and seeds, reserving any juices, then chop the flesh.

Put the oil into a frying pan, heat gently, then add the garlic and sauté for 3 minutes. Add the tomatoes, chilli flakes and oregano and simmer gently for 15 minutes. Stir in the peppers and the vinegar and simmer for a further 5 minutes to evaporate any excess liquid.

Transfer to a blender and purée until fairly smooth. Add salt and pepper to taste and let cool. It may be stored in a screw-top jar in the refrigerator for up to 3 days.

Put the crushed peppercorns onto a large plate. Brush the tuna steaks with oil, then press the crushed peppercorns into the surface. Preheat a stove-top grill pan or barbecue until hot, add the tuna and cook for 1 minute on each side. Wrap loosely in foil and let rest for 5 minutes before serving with the salsa rossa and a salad of mixed leaves.

meat and poultry

The barbecue is my favourite way of cooking meat for al fresco dining, and I like to marinate it overnight beforehand so the flavours penetrate deeply. Such age-old methods of flavouring and tenderizing meat can be found in India, the Middle East, Indonesia, Thailand and Japan: every cuisine provides similar delicious recipes, as this chapter will show.

For the outdoor cook, skewered meats are ideal. They're easy to prepare, quick to cook (and delicious to eat). However, no recipe book for eating outdoors would be complete without the two great classics; barbecued pork spareribs and the beef burger.

When cooking outdoors, remember that food takes longer to cook on a barbecue than on top of the stove or in the oven. Remove marinated foods from the refrigerator about an hour before cooking to let them return to room temperature. That way, they'll cook properly and won't be underdone in the middle. One hour before you begin cooking, start preparing the barbecue. If using charcoal, light the coals and heat for 40–45 minutes. The coals should have passed the red-hot phase and become lightly covered with ash before you add the food, so it will cook properly without burning on the outside.

orange and soy **glazed duck**

This is a great dish when you are short of time – it is quick to cook and tastes delicious. Serve the duck breasts with your choice of vegetables such as steamed Chinese leaves, bok choy (also known as pak choi), steamed broccoli or sautéed spinach.

4 duck breast fillets, about 250 g each

juice of 1 orange

3 tablespoons dark soy sauce

2 tablespoons maple syrup

½ teaspoon Chinese five-spice powder

2 garlic cloves, crushed

freshly ground Szechuan peppercorns or black pepper

To serve

steamed broccoli or bok choy, or sautéed spinach

1 orange, cut into wedges

Serves 4

Using a sharp knife, score the fat on each duck breast crossways several times. Put the breasts into a shallow dish.

Put the orange juice, soy sauce, maple syrup, Chinese five-spice powder, garlic and pepper into a small jug or bowl, mix well, then pour the mixture over the fillets. Cover with clingfilm and marinate in the refrigerator for as long as possible. You can leave them overnight, but return them to room temperature for 1 hour before cooking.

Heat a stove-top grill pan until hot, add the duck breasts, skin side down, and sear for 1–2 minutes. Transfer to a roasting tin, adding the marinade juices. Cook the duck in a preheated oven at 200°C (400°F) Gas 6 for about 10 minutes or until medium rare. Remove the duck from the oven, wrap it in foil and keep it warm for 5 minutes.

Pour the juices from the roasting tin into a small saucepan and, using a large spoon, very carefully skim the fat off the surface. Transfer the pan to the top of the stove and bring the juices to the boil for 2 minutes, until thickened slightly. Serve the duck breasts sprinkled with the juices and accompanied by broccoli, bok choy or spinach and wedges of orange.

duck yakitori

6 tablespoons Japanese soy sauce

3 tablespoons sake

2 tablespoons caster sugar

4 small duck breast fillets, about 150 g each, skinned

soba noodles, cooked according to the packet instructions, then drained and chilled, to serve

Cucumber salad

2 tablespoons rice vinegar

2 tablespoons caster sugar

½ cucumber, about 20 cm, finely sliced

1 red chilli, deseeded and chopped

8 bamboo skewers soaked in warm water for 30 minutes

Serves 4

Put the soy sauce, sake and sugar into a small saucepan and heat gently to dissolve the sugar. Cool completely.

Cut the duck lengthways into 3 mm strips and put into a shallow dish. Pour over the soy sauce mixture and marinate in the refrigerator for 2–4 hours or overnight.

Just before cooking the duck, prepare the salad. Put the vinegar, sugar and 2 tablespoons water into a small saucepan, heat to dissolve the sugar, then let cool. Stir in the cucumber and chilli and set aside.

Thread the duck strips onto skewers, zigzagging back and forth. Cook on a preheated barbecue or under a grill for 2 minutes on each side until cooked through. Serve with chilled soba noodles and the cucumber salad.

chicken kebabs
moroccan-style

500 g chicken breast fillets, skinned

2 tablespoons extra virgin olive oil

freshly squeezed juice of 1 large lemon

1 tablespoon chopped fresh thyme leaves

2 garlic cloves, crushed

1 teaspoon ground turmeric

1 teaspoon ground cinnamon

½ teaspoon ground allspice

½ teaspoon salt

¼ teaspoon ground cayenne

To serve

lemon wedges

plain yoghurt

8 bamboo skewers soaked in warm water for 30 minutes

Serves 4

Cut the chicken lengthways into 3 mm strips and put into a shallow ceramic dish. Put the oil, lemon juice, thyme, garlic, turmeric, cinnamon, allspice, salt and cayenne into a jug, mix well, then pour over the chicken.

Cover and marinate overnight in the refrigerator.

The next day, return to room temperature for 1 hour. Thread the strips onto skewers, zigzagging back and forth. Cook on a preheated barbecue or stove-top grill pan for 3–4 minutes on each side until charred and cooked through. Serve with lemon wedges and yoghurt.

Ever since I first discovered Japanese food, I have been a huge fan, especially of the pungent flavours of skewered teriyaki and yakitori. The rich sauce copes perfectly with the gamy taste of duck and tenderizes the flesh beautifully. The Moroccan version is, of course, the kebab and is wondrously flavoured with scented North African spices.

chicken 'panini'
with mozzarella

'Panini' is the Italian word for little sandwiches, usually toasted. Here, instead of bread, we are toasting (or barbecuing) a chicken breast fillet stuffed with basil and mozzarella – melted, gooey and delicious!

Cut the mozzarella into 8 thick slices and set aside.

Put the chicken breasts onto a board and, using a sharp knife, cut horizontally through the thickness without cutting all the way through. Open out flat and season the insides with a little salt and pepper.

Put 2 basil leaves, a few garlic slices and 2 slices of cheese into each breast, then fold back over, pressing firmly together. Secure with cocktail sticks.

Brush the parcels with a little oil and cook on a preheated barbecue or stove-top grill pan for about 8 minutes on each side until the cheese is beginning to ooze at the sides. Serve hot with the salsa rossa and sprinkle with a few basil leaves.

250 g mozzarella cheese

4 large, skinless, boneless chicken breasts

8 large basil leaves

2 garlic cloves, sliced thinly

1 tablespoon olive oil

sea salt and freshly ground black pepper

To serve

salsa rossa (page 88)

basil leaves

Serves 4

barbecued mexican-style **poussins**

Spatchcocked poussins are ideally suited to barbecue cooking, as the process of opening them out flat ensures quick and even cooking. The marinade ingredients have a Mexican flavour and work particularly well accompanied by the creamy corn salsa on page 41.

4 poussins

creamy corn salsa, to serve
(page 41)

Mexican marinade

4 jalapeño chillies

8 garlic cloves, peeled

4 tablespoons orange juice

2 tablespoons lime juice

1 tablespoon ground cumin

1 tablespoon dried oregano
or thyme

2 teaspoons salt

6 tablespoons olive oil

1 tablespoon maple syrup or
clear honey

Serves 4

To spatchcock the poussins, turn them breast side down and, using poultry shears or sturdy scissors, cut down each side of the backbone and discard it. Turn the birds over and open them out flat, pressing down hard on the breastbone. Thread 2 skewers diagonally through each poussin from the wings to the thigh bones.

To make the marinade, skewer the chillies and garlic together and cook on a preheated medium-hot barbecue or under a grill for 10 minutes, turning frequently, until evenly browned. Scrape off and discard the skins from the chillies and chop the flesh coarsely. Put the flesh and seeds into a food processor, add the garlic and all the remaining marinade ingredients and blend to a purée.

Pour the marinade over the poussins and let marinate in the refrigerator overnight. Return them to room temperature for 1 hour before cooking

When ready to cook, remove the birds from their marinade and barbecue over medium-hot preheated coals for 12 minutes on each side, basting occasionally. Remove from the heat, let rest for 5 minutes, then serve with the creamy corn salsa.

chicken caesar **wrap**

This salad has travelled all over the world and many additions to the basic lettuce and croutons with cheese and anchovy dressing can be found. Recently, I saw 'Caesar Salad Wrap' on offer at a sandwich shop: I thought it would be a great idea for a picnic dish.

Grill or fry the bacon for 2–3 minutes until crisp. Cool, then cut into thin strips. Roughly shred the chicken into large strips.

To make the dressing, put the egg yolk into a small bowl, add the lemon juice, Worcestershire sauce and a little salt and pepper and whisk until frothy. Gradually whisk in the oil, a little at a time, until thickened and glossy. Add 2 tablespoons water to thin the sauce, then stir in the cheese.

Lay the tortilla flat on a work surface and arrange a little lettuce down the middle of each one. Top with chicken, bacon, anchovies, a spoonful of the dressing and, finally, more lettuce. Wrap the tortilla into a roll, then wrap the roll in a napkin. Repeat to make 6 wraps. Serve immediately or chill to serve later.

3 large slices of smoked bacon

250 g cooked chicken breast

6 small flour tortillas

300 g cos lettuce, shredded (inner leaves only)

12 anchovy fillets in oil, drained and chopped

Caesar dressing

1 egg yolk

1 tablespoon lemon juice

1 teaspoon Worcestershire sauce

150 ml olive oil

25 g freshly grated Parmesan cheese

sea salt and freshly ground black pepper

Serves 6

tex-mex **pork rack**

2 racks barbecue pork spareribs,
500 g each

Sweet chilli marinade

2 garlic cloves, crushed

2 tablespoons sea salt

2 tablespoons ground cumin

2 teaspoons chilli powder

1 teaspoon dried oregano

8 tablespoons maple syrup
or golden syrup

4 tablespoons red wine vinegar

4 tablespoons olive oil

Serves 4–6

Wash the ribs and pat them dry with kitchen paper.
Transfer to a shallow, non-metal dish.

Put all the marinade ingredients into a bowl, mix well,
pour over the ribs, then work in well with your hands.
Cover and let marinate overnight in the refrigerator.

The next day, return the ribs to room temperature
for 1 hour, then cook on a preheated medium-hot
barbecue for about 30 minutes, turning and basting
frequently with the marinade juices. Cool a little, then
serve with chilli-spiked cornbread (right).

chilli spiked **cornbread**

150 g medium cornmeal

150 g plain flour

1½ teaspoons salt

1 tablespoon baking powder

2 eggs, beaten

250 ml milk

2 tablespoons olive oil

2 large red chillies, deseeded and
chopped

200 g canned corn kernels, drained

25 g finely grated Cheddar cheese

2 tablespoons chopped fresh coriander

*a cake tin, 20 cm square, greased and
base-lined with baking parchment*

Serves 8

Put the cornmeal, flour, salt and baking powder into a
bowl and mix. Make a well in the centre and pour in the
eggs, milk and olive oil. Beat with a wooden spoon to
make a smooth batter.

Fold in the chillies, corn, cheese and coriander, then
spoon into the prepared cake tin. Bake in a preheated
oven at 200°C (400°F) Gas 6 for 25 minutes, or until a
skewer inserted in the centre comes out clean.

Remove from the oven and let cool in the tin for about
5 minutes, then turn out onto a wire rack to cool
completely. Serve cut into squares.

mini **pork and apple pies**

250 g pork fillet, diced

125 g pork belly, diced

75 g smoked bacon, diced

25 g chicken livers

1 small onion, minced

1 tablespoon chopped sage

1 small garlic clove, crushed

a pinch of ground nutmeg

1 red apple, peeled, cored and diced

salt and black pepper

Pastry

300 g plain flour, plus extra for kneading

1½ teaspoons salt

60 g white vegetable fat

Glaze

1 egg yolk

1 tablespoon milk

1 jam jar

6 pieces of wax paper, about 30 x 7 cm

a baking sheet

Serves 6

Put the pork fillet, pork belly, bacon and chicken livers into a food processor and blend briefly to mince the meat. Transfer to a bowl and mix in the onion, sage, garlic, mace or nutmeg and a little salt and pepper. Set aside.

To make the pastry, sift the flour and salt into a bowl. Put the fat and 150 ml water into a saucepan and heat gently until the fat melts and the water comes to the boil. Pour the liquid into the flour and, using a wooden spoon, gently draw the flour into the liquid to form a soft dough.

Let cool for a few minutes and, as soon as the dough is cool enough to handle, knead lightly in the bowl until smooth.

Divide the dough into 8 and roll out 6 of these on a lightly floured surface to form discs 12 cm across. Carefully invert them, one at a time over an upturned jam jar. Wrap a piece of waxed paper around the outside, then tie around the middle with kitchen string.

Turn the whole thing over so the pastry is sitting flat. Carefully work the jar up and out of the pastry shell (you may need to slip a small palette knife down between the pastry and the jar, to loosen it).

Divide the pork filling into 6 portions and put 1 portion into each pie. Put the diced apple on top. Roll out the remaining 2 pieces of dough and cut 3 rounds from each piece with a pastry cutter, the same size as the top of the pies.

Put a pastry round on top of each pie, press the edges together to seal, then turn the edges inwards and over to form a rim.

To make the glaze, put the egg yolk and milk into a bowl, beat well, then brush over the tops of the pies. Pierce each one with a fork to let the steam escape. Transfer to a large baking sheet and cook in a preheated oven at 190°C (375°F) Gas 5 for 45–50 minutes until golden. Remove from the oven, transfer to a wire rack, let cool and serve cold with a green salad.

thai-style **beef salad**

1 tablespoon Szechuan peppercorns, or black peppercorns, lightly crushed

1 teaspoon ground coriander

1 teaspoon sea salt

500 g beef fillet, in the piece

1 tablespoon peanut or vegetable oil

1 cucumber, finely sliced

4 spring onions, finely sliced

2 baby bok choy, finely sliced

a handful of Thai basil

a handful of mint

a handful of coriander leaves

Lime dressing

15 g palm sugar or brown sugar

1 tablespoon fish sauce

2 tablespoons lime juice

2 red chillies, deseeded and chopped

1 garlic clove, crushed

Serves 4

What I love about many Thai dishes (as well as Vietnamese and Indonesian) is their use of fresh herbs. Many of their salads, soups and stews are flooded with the pungent flavours of Thai basil, mint and coriander. Thai basil is available from Asian stores, but you could use ordinary basil instead. Bok choy is also known as 'pak choi' in some places.

Put the peppercorns, ground coriander and salt onto a plate and mix. Rub the beef all over with the oil and then put onto the plate and turn to coat with the spices.

Cook the beef on a preheated barbecue or stove-top grill pan for about 10 minutes, turning to brown evenly. Remove from the heat and let cool.

Meanwhile, to make the dressing, put the sugar into a saucepan, add the fish sauce and 2 tablespoons water and heat until the sugar dissolves. Let cool, then stir in the lime juice, chillies and garlic.

Cut the beef into thin slices and put into a large bowl. Add the cucumber, spring onions, bok choy and herbs. Pour over the dressing, toss well, then serve.

best-ever **beef burger**

*There are many burger recipes and everyone
has their favourite – this one is very good.
I always serve it in a bun, with pickles and
sauce and a simple salad of tomatoes, lettuce
and olives.*

750 g sirloin steak, minced*

50 g skinless pork belly,
minced*

8 anchovy fillets in oil,
drained and finely chopped

50 g fresh white
breadcrumbs

2 tablespoons chopped
fresh thyme

1 tablespoon wholegrain
mustard

1 large egg, lightly beaten

sea salt and freshly ground
black pepper

To serve

hamburger buns

fried onions

dill pickles (gherkins)

tomato, lettuce and olive
salad (optional)

Serves 6

Put the minced steak and pork into a bowl and add the
anchovies, breadcrumbs, thyme, mustard, beaten egg,
salt and pepper, working it with your hands to make a
nice, sticky mixture.

Shape into 6 burgers and chill for 1 hour. Cook on a
preheated barbecue or in a lightly oiled frying pan for
about 4 minutes on each side. Remove from the heat
and let rest for 5 minutes. Serve in a bun, with fried
onions, dill pickles and the tomato, lettuce and olive
salad, if using.

*Note To make the burger mince, ask your butcher to
put the beef and pork through a meat mincer.
Alternatively, put it into a food processor and pulse
briefly to make a slightly coarse mince.

I once worked in a London wine bar, where one of the regular dishes on the menu was a fillet steak topped with a slice of blue cheese butter. It was very popular with the diners (and the staff, too) – this is my interpretation.

steak with blue cheese butter

To make the blue cheese butter, put the butter, cheese, walnuts and parsley into a bowl and beat well. Season to taste. Form into a log, wrap in foil and chill for about 30 minutes.

Lightly season the steaks and cook on a preheated barbecue (or pan-fry in a little oil) for 3 minutes on each side for rare, or 4–5 minutes for medium to well done.

Cut the butter into 8 slices. Put 2 slices of butter onto each cooked steak, wrap loosely with foil and let rest for 5 minutes.

Serve the steaks with a salad of baby spinach.

4 fillet steaks, 200 g each

sea salt and freshly ground black pepper

baby spinach salad, to serve

Blue cheese butter

50 g unsalted butter, softened

50 g soft blue cheese, such as Gorgonzola

25 g walnuts, finely ground in a blender

2 tablespoons chopped fresh parsley

sea salt and freshly ground black pepper

Serves 4

Souvlaki is the classic Greek kebab, a delicious combination of cubed lamb marinated in red wine with herbs and lemon juice. The meat is tenderized by the wine, resulting in a juicy and succulent dish.

souvlaki with cracked wheat salad

Trim any large pieces of fat from the lamb and then cut the meat into 2.5 cm cubes. Put into a shallow, non-metal dish. Add the rosemary, oregano, onion, garlic, wine, lemon juice, olive oil, salt and pepper. Toss well, cover and let marinate in the refrigerator for 4 hours. Return to room temperature for 1 hour before cooking.

To make the salad, soak the cracked wheat in warm water for 30 minutes until the water has been absorbed and the grains have softened. Strain well to extract any excess water and transfer the wheat to a bowl. Add all the remaining ingredients, season to taste and set aside for 30 minutes to develop the flavours.

Thread the lamb onto large rosemary stalks or metal skewers. Cook on a preheated barbecue or under a grill for 10 minutes, turning and basting from time to time. Let rest for 5 minutes, then serve with the salad.

1 kg neck end of lamb

1 tablespoon chopped fresh rosemary

1 tablespoon dried oregano

1 onion, chopped

4 garlic cloves, chopped

300 ml red wine

juice of 1 lemon

75 ml olive oil

salt and pepper

Cracked wheat salad

350 g cracked wheat (bulghur wheat)

25 g fresh parsley

15 g fresh mint leaves

2 garlic cloves, crushed

150 ml olive oil

juice of 2 lemons

a pinch of caster sugar

salt and pepper

6 large rosemary stalks or metal skewers

Serves 6

butterflied lamb with indian spices

'Butterfly' is the term used when a piece of meat or fish is opened out flat. When preparing a leg of lamb, the bone is removed so the meat can be laid out flat, so it will cook quickly and evenly. It's easy to do, but you can also ask your butcher to do it for you.

1.5 kg leg of lamb, butterflied

1 onion, chopped

4 garlic cloves, chopped

1 tablespoon grated fresh ginger

1 cinnamon stick, coarsely crumbled

1 tablespoon coriander seeds

2 teaspoons cumin seeds

¼ teaspoon whole cloves

1 tablespoon curry powder

2 tablespoons tomato paste

2 tablespoons peanut or sunflower oil, plus extra for brushing

sea salt and freshly ground black pepper

To serve

Indian breads, such as naan or chapattis, or pita bread

plain yoghurt

sprigs of coriander

Serves 6–8

To butterfly the lamb, turn to the side of the leg where the bone is closest to the surface. Using a sharp knife, cut down the length of the bone, then run your knife close to the bone, using small cuts, to separate the bone from the flesh. Remove and discard the bone.

Open out the butterflied lamb and cut several shallow slashes in each side.

Put the onion, garlic and ginger into a food processor and work to a smooth paste. Transfer to a bowl.

Put the cinnamon stick, coriander and cumin seeds and cloves into a dry frying pan and heat gently until lightly browned and aromatic. Cool slightly, then grind to a powder in a spice grinder or with a mortar and pestle. Add to the onion paste, then stir in the curry powder, tomato paste, oil, salt and pepper.

Spread this paste all over the lamb, cover and let marinate overnight in the refrigerator. Return to room temperature for about 1 hour before cooking.

When ready to cook, scrape off the excess marinade, brush the lamb with a little oil and put on the barbecue rack over medium-hot coals. Cook for 12–15 minutes on each side until the outside is charred (leaving the centre beautifully pink). Remove the lamb from the heat and let it rest for 10 minutes before carving.

Serve the lamb with Indian breads, plain yoghurt and a few sprigs of coriander.

sweet things

Summer is prime time for fruit, so who can avoid the temptation to serve it ripe and sweet and full of flavour, churned into ice creams, as toppings for puddings such as a sweet cloud of meringue, or baked into cakes or tarts.

The simplest way of course is in a fruit salad. Make sure the fruit is ripe and good, then just sprinkle with a little sugar and perhaps liqueur and serve as it is   or perhaps with a dab of cream or a scoop of ice cream.

Chocolate is, naturally, in a class of its own – the only concern in summer is that it might melt first, before you have a chance to have it melt in your mouth. My refrigerator chocolate cake is the answer!

Most of us have a sweet tooth and perhaps it's even sweeter when indulged outdoors. Even on a picnic, it's essential to pack a cake, a sweet tart or even ice cream to round off a wonderful meal. Ice cream may seem a little ambitious for a picnic, but, provided you have a good cool box with plenty of ice packs, it should be safe for a couple of hours before it succumbs to meltdown. I usually wrap the container in newspaper for extra insulation.

fresh figs with vin santo and mascarpone

250 g mascarpone cheese

25–50 g icing sugar, or to taste

6 tablespoons Vin Santo, plus extra to serve

12 ripe figs

Serves 6

This lovely, simple dish is best served when you can find very good quality fresh figs, preferably straight from the tree. Vin Santo is an Italian sweet wine that marries well with the flavour of both the figs and the mascarpone – if you can't find it, you could also use port or a cream sherry.

Put the mascarpone into a bowl, add the icing sugar and Vin Santo and beat until smooth. Set aside to infuse for 30 minutes, then transfer to a small serving bowl.

Cut the figs in half and arrange on a large serving platter with the bowl of mascarpone. Serve with the bottle of Vin Santo for people to help themselves.

meringues with rosewater cream

3 egg whites

175 g caster sugar

¼ teaspoon ground cardamom

200 ml double cream

1 tablespoon clear honey

1 tablespoon rosewater

pomegranate seeds, to serve (optional)

a baking sheet lined with baking parchment

Serves 6

Rosewater is an exotic, fragrant aromatic widely used in Middle Eastern and North African cooking. It's sold in delicatessens and the baking section of supermarkets. The meringues and rosewater cream are particularly good served with fresh pomegranate seeds, but work equally well with other fruits such as cherries, nectarines or peaches.

Put the egg whites into a clean, dry bowl and whisk until they start to peak. Gradually whisk in the sugar, a spoonful at a time, until the mixture becomes very thick and glossy. Fold in the ground cardamom.

Drop 12 spoonfuls of the meringue mixture onto the prepared baking sheet, leaving a gap between each mound. Bake in a preheated oven at 160°C (325°F) Gas 3 for 1 hour. Remove from the oven, transfer the meringues to a wire rack and let cool.

Put the cream, honey and rosewater into a bowl and whip until the mixture just holds its shape. Put a couple of spoonfuls of the whipped cream into each bowl, add the meringues and top with the pomegranate seeds, if using.

caramelized **plum sorbet**

A refreshing and summery sorbet – pretty and delicious when served with thin, crisp, almond biscuits. Roasting the plums before they are puréed will intensify their flavour.

1 kg red plums, halved and pitted

2 tablespoons caster sugar

freshly squeezed juice of ½ lemon

sweet almond wafer biscuits, to serve (optional)

Sugar syrup

300 ml sugar

1 vanilla pod, split lengthways

serves 6–8

Put the halved plums, cut side up, into a baking dish, sprinkle with the sugar, and bake in a preheated oven at 200°C (400°F) Gas 6 for 20 minutes until golden and softened. Let cool completely, then transfer to a blender and purée until very smooth. Stir in the lemon juice.

Meanwhile, to make the sugar syrup, put the sugar and vanilla pod into a saucepan, add 600 ml water, and heat gently until the sugar has dissolved. Bring to the boil, reduce the heat and simmer for 5 minutes. Let cool, remove the vanilla pod, then stir the syrup into the plum purée.

Transfer to an ice cream maker and churn, according to the manufacturer's instructions. Store in the freezer until required.

Alternatively, transfer the purée to a plastic container and freeze for 5 hours, beating at hourly intervals with a balloon whisk. (This will break down the ice crystals and make the sorbet smooth.) Serve with the almond biscuits, if using.

toasted coconut ice cream
with grilled pineapple

Toasting the desiccated coconut enriches the ice cream and gives it a lovely nutty flavour. Although in this recipe I serve it with wedges of barbecued pineapple, it works equally well with other fruits such as mango or peaches.

To make the ice cream, put the coconut into a dry frying pan and toast, stirring over medium heat for 2–3 minutes until evenly browned. Transfer to a saucepan, then add the cream, coconut milk and sugar. Heat gently until it just reaches boiling point.

Put the egg yolks into a bowl and beat with a wooden spoon until pale. Stir in about 2 tablespoons of the hot custard, then return the mixture to the pan. Heat gently, stirring constantly until the mixture thickens enough to coat the back of the wooden spoon. Remove the pan from the heat and let cool completely.

When cold, strain the custard and freeze in an ice cream maker according to the manufacturer's instructions. Transfer to the freezer until required.

Alternatively, pour the cold custard into a plastic container and freeze for 5 hours, beating at hourly intervals with a balloon whisk.

To prepare the pineapple, cut it lengthways into wedges (including the leafy top) and remove the core sections. Put the sugar, butter and rum into a small saucepan and heat until the sugar dissolves. Brush a little of the mixture over the pineapple wedges, then cook them on a preheated barbecue or on a stove-top grill pan for 2 minutes on each side until charred and tender. Remove from the heat and, holding the flesh with a fork, cut between the skin and flesh with a sharp knife. Cut the flesh into segments to make it easier to eat, then reassemble the wedges. Serve with the ice cream and remaining rum sauce, about 2 tablespoons each.

1 pineapple, medium or small, with leafy top if possible

100 g soft brown sugar

100 g unsalted butter

100 ml dark rum

Ice cream

25 g desiccated coconut

450 ml double cream

300 ml coconut milk

100 g caster sugar

5 egg yolks

Serves 6

pear gingerbread

500 g self-rising flour

1 tablespoon ground ginger

½ teaspoon bicarbonate of soda

½ teaspoon salt

175 g light soft brown sugar

175 g unsalted butter

175 g black treacle

175 g golden syrup

300 ml milk

1 egg, lightly beaten

2 large pears, peeled, cored and diced

*a baking tin, 30 x 20 cm, greased
and base-lined with baking parchment*

Serves 12

Sift the flour, ginger, bicarbonate of soda and salt into
a large bowl. Put the sugar, butter, treacle, golden syrup
and milk into a saucepan and heat gently until the
butter has melted and the sugar has dissolved.

Pour into the flour mixture, then add the egg and beat
with a wooden spoon until smooth. Fold in the diced
pears, then spoon onto the prepared baking tin.

Transfer to a preheated oven and bake at 160°C
(325°F) Gas 3 for 1½ hours, or until a skewer inserted
into the centre comes out clean. Cool in the tin for
10 minutes, then let cool on a wire rack before serving.

The cooled cake may be wrapped in foil and stored in
an airtight container for up to 5 days.

refrigerator
chocolate cake

400 g dark chocolate

125 g unsalted butter

200 g digestive biscuits, coarsely crushed

50 g pine nuts

50 g shelled pistachio nuts, coarsely chopped

100 g crystallized ginger, coarsely chopped

50 g cocoa powder

1 teaspoon ground cinnamon

icing sugar, to dust (optional)

*a springform cake tin, 23 cm diameter,
greased and base-lined with baking parchment*

Serves 12

Put the chocolate and butter into a bowl set over a
saucepan of gently simmering water and heat gently
until melted. Stir in all the remaining ingredients except
the icing sugar, then spoon into the prepared cake tin.
Press the mixture well into the base and sides of the
tin and smooth the surface with a palette knife. Cover
with foil and chill overnight in the refrigerator.

When ready to serve, carefully work around the edges
of the cake with the palette knife and unmould onto a
board, removing the paper from the base. Dust with
icing sugar, if using, and serve in thin fingers.

The cake may be stored in the refrigerator for up to
3 days.

lemon cake with vanilla syrup and strawberries

Vanilla syrup transforms this cake into a lovely pudding, but you can also serve it simply with a spoonful of yoghurt.

125 g unsalted butter, softened

125 g caster sugar

2 lemons

2 eggs, lightly beaten

200 g self-raising flour

50 g fine semolina

150 ml full-fat yoghurt

fresh strawberries, to serve

Vanilla syrup

150 g caster sugar

1 vanilla pod

a springform cake tin, 23 cm diameter, greased and base-lined with baking parchment

Serves 6

Grate the zest and squeeze the juice from the lemons. Put the butter, sugar and lemon zest into a bowl and whisk until pale and soft. Gradually beat in the eggs, a little at a time, until evenly mixed. Fold in the flour and semolina, then stir in the yoghurt and lemon juice.

Spoon the mixture into the prepared cake tin and bake in a preheated oven at 180°C (350°F) Gas 4 for about 40 minutes until risen and spongy. The cake is cooked when a skewer inserted into the middle of the cake comes out clean. Cool in the tin for about 5 minutes, then turn out onto a wire rack to cool completely.

Meanwhile, to make the syrup, split the vanilla bean lengthways. Put the sugar and vanilla pod into a small saucepan and add 300 ml water. Heat gently until the sugar has dissolved. Bring to the boil and simmer for about 5 minutes until it becomes syrupy. Remove from the heat and let cool a little.

To serve, cut the cake into slices while still slightly warm, pour over the syrup and serve with strawberries.

drinks

No outdoor feast can be enjoyed without a tipple or two. Not that they have to be alcohol-based: cool smoothies and iced tea and coffee are all perfect. Remember, although smoothies are best immediately after blending, you can make them in advance and give them a good shake up before drinking.

If you're having a large party, but don't want to serve just wine and you don't have the manpower to prepare stick drinks and other cocktails en masse, try punch-style drinks such as Planter's Punch, summery Pimms, wine-based sangrias, or the endlessly popular Bloody Mary made in a big jug that can be constantly replenished.

What is a must, however, is the chill factor – serving lukewarm drinks on a hot day is no fun at all. If you're having a barbecue, organize big tubs of ice to take the drinks. If you're going on a picnic, pack the coolbox with a bag of ice cubes, then put the drinks on top. If you're having a large party, hire extra freezers for ice and refrigerators for drinks, plus lots of glassware, allowing spares so you don't have to wash up in the middle of the party. Ask for the drinks to be delivered already cold, because it can take a long time to chill a large quantity of drinks or to freeze ice yourself. Then chill out, al fresco!

iced ginger tea

When making iced tea, it's best to add the tea bags to cold water rather than boiling water in order to avoid the unpleasant scum that can appear on the surface. So boil the water, then let it cool before adding the tea.

50 g fresh ginger, peeled and
finely sliced
4 tea bags (I prefer Indian tea)
2 limes, sliced
ice cubes
lemonade

Serves 6

Put the sliced ginger into a large jug, pour over 1 litre boiling water and leave until cold. Add the tea bags and chill for 1 hour.

Strain the tea into a clean jug, add the slices of lime and ice cubes, then top up with lemonade.

iced lemon coffee

Iced lemon coffee can be just as refreshing as as iced lemon tea on a hot day. It may sound a little strange, but it's very thirst-quenching.

500 ml freshly brewed espresso coffee
caster sugar, to taste
ice cubes
1 tablespoon freshly squeezed
lemon juice
lemon peel, to serve

Serves 6

Pour the coffee into a large jug, add sugar to taste and stir until dissolved. Let cool, then chill until very cold.

Half-fill glasses with ice cubes. Add the lemon juice to the coffee, then pour into the glasses and serve with a twist of lemon peel.

strawberry and banana
ice cream shake

A great shake for those times when you're in serious ice cream mode. Other fruits also marry well with the banana – try mango and banana with vanilla ice cream or raspberry and banana with raspberry ice cream.

250 g ripe strawberries, hulled

1 ripe banana, peeled and chopped

4 scoops strawberry ice cream, plus extra to serve (optional)

200 ml milk

Serves 3–4

Put the strawberries, banana, ice cream and milk into a blender and purée until very smooth. Pour into glasses and serve topped with extra ice cream, if using.

lemonade with mint and bitters

A delightfully simple drink, ideal for hot summer days. The Bitters give the lemonade a refreshing, herbal flavour and make it a pretty pale pink.

1 litre lemonade

6 sprigs of mint

Angostura Bitters

lemon slices

ice cubes

Serves 6

Pour the lemonade into 6 tall glasses, adding a sprig of mint to each one. Add a few drops of Bitters, a few slices of lemon and ice cubes, then serve at once.

stick drinks

Stick drinks, also known as caprioskas, are cocktails made by mashing fruits and sugar together with a stick, usually a lollipop stick, or, as I prefer, a citrus press. You can use almost any fruit as long as you include chopped limes and sugar. These are two of my favourites.

lime and mint stick drink

12 large mint leaves
2 teaspoons brown sugar
1 lime, finely diced, including skin
ice cubes
2 large shots Bacardi rum
soda water

cocktail shaker or jug
2 cocktail glasses

Serves 2

Put the mint leaves, sugar and lime into a shaker or jug and mash with a stick or spoon until quite pulpy. Alternatively, use a mortar and pestle.

Fill 2 glasses with ice to chill them thoroughly, then tip the ice into the mashed mint mixture. Add the Bacardi to the mixture, shake well, then pour back into the glasses. Add a little soda water and serve.

kiwifruit, passionfruit and lime sticky

1 large lime, diced
1 large kiwifruit, peeled and diced
12 mint leaves
3 teaspoons caster sugar
1 large passionfruit, halved
ice cubes
2 large shots vodka

cocktail shaker or jug
2 cocktail glasses

Serves 2

Put the lime and kiwifruit into a shaker or jug, add the mint, sugar and passionfruit pulp and seeds. Mash well until pulpy.

Fill 2 glasses with ice to chill them thoroughly, then tip the ice into the kiwifruit mixture. Add the vodka, shake or stir well, then pour back into the glasses.

outdoor parties

A drinks party can be an exercise in logistics. If your party is outdoors, here are a few things to keep in mind:

Food
• Serve 4–6 canapes per person, per hour.
• Keep food hot or cold: danger zone is 4–65°C and the most dangerous is about 30°C, the temperature of a hot kitchen!
• If people are juggling a drink, a plate and a napkin, make it easy – serve foods they can eat with their fingers or a fork.

Drinks
• Better too much than too little – most suppliers will let you return what you don't use – and don't forget the non-drinkers.
Champagne For a 2-hour party, allow ½ bottle each, ¾ bottle for 3 hours (6 glasses in a bottle, or 8 if making cocktails).
Wine 1 bottle per person (serve the leftovers at your next dinner party). In summer, allow 3 bottles of white to 1 of red.
Spirits and cocktails 16 measures in a 750 ml bottle of spirits. Allow 3 per person during a 2-hour party.
Punches Strong punches, such as Planter's Punch, contain about the same amount of alcohol as a measure of spirits, so cater as for spirits. Wine-based punches, such as sangria, are only a little weaker than wine, so cater as for wine.
Mineral water and soft drinks Don't forget the non-drinkers, 'designated drivers' and kids. Have lots and keep it cold.

PARTY COUNTDOWN

One week ahead
• Order drinks, glasses, ice, ice buckets and bins for ice, drinks and rubbish.
• Arrange shade, music, candles and insect repellent.
• Organize kitchen equipment for your chosen menu – hire extra freezers and refrigerators if necessary.
• Prepare dishes to be frozen until the day.

Two or three days ahead
• Prepare ice creams, wrap cakes, buy ready-to-roll pastry.
• Check with suppliers and caterers.

One day ahead
• Buy all the food, except the most perishable.
• Prepare meats, sauces and marinades and chill overnight.
• Assemble skewers, keeping bamboo skewers wet until ready to cook.
• Cook dishes such as cold meats to be chilled overnight.
• Prepare basic mixtures for drinks such as punch.
• Arrange seating and tables, check linen and napkins and collect bar equipment indoors (corkscrews, glasses, etc.)
• Put the drinks in the refrigerator to chill.

Morning of party
• Buy foods such as salad leaves, herbs, cream, etc.
• Prepare dressings and salsas.
• Prepare vegetables and cover with clingfilm.
• Assemble any dishes that are able to stand, then cover and chill.

One hour ahead
• Assemble and cook all dishes except those needing last-minute cooking.
• If any of the food is going to be barbecued, light the coals – they should be at the right temperature in about 40–45 minutes.

Thirty minutes ahead
• Preheat the oven, uncork still wines, prepare materials for cocktails.

the best barbecue

Barbecues come in all shapes, sizes, varieties and prices, from small disposable aluminium grills sold in supermarkets, to large, high-tech covered gas or electric grills. Some barbecues have both a grill and a flat plate offering versatility, but this is not essential. A windshield is a great advantage.

Cooking on a charcoal barbecue
• Charcoal barbecues use either standard briquettes or hardwood lump charcoal. The former may contain chemicals from the process used to make them, which, though totally safe, may affect the flavour of the food. I prefer hardwood lump charcoal, which, though not as readily available, contains no additives, burns easily, gets far hotter and lasts longer.
• Arrange the fuel at least 10 cm deep in as large an area as possible, leaving a little room around the edges.
• Put a few barbecue lighters in between the coals and light them with a taper or matches.
• Let the coals burn for about 40–45 minutes until all the flames have subsided and the coals are covered in grey ash. To test the heat, hold your hand about 12 cm above the fire and count how long it can stay there. A hot fire will be a couple of seconds, a medium-hot fire 3–4 seconds and a cool fire 5–6 seconds. Many barbecues have adjustable rungs: the closest to the heat is obviously the hottest.

Cooking on gas or electric barbecues
• For proper browning, preheat until very hot before adding the food, then reduce the heat as necessary.
• They can be adjusted in the same way as a domestic cooker, by turning the temperature up or down.
• They are often available with a hood, to cover the food as it grills (a similar effect to roasting).

Portable barbecues
• A wide selection of styles is available, fueled by either charcoal or gas. Remember, coals stay hot for some time, so dispose of them legally and safely, or wait until they are totally cold before carefully packing them in a bag to take with you.
• Set up on level ground and never move a barbecue once lit.
• Safety is extremely important: in some places, barbecues will constitute a fire risk. Be sensible and set up the barbecue away from dry timber or grass and always take a fire blanket or a small portable fire extinguisher with you.

Cleaning
• Clean the grill as soon as possible after cooking, while it is still assembled and any residual bits of food stuck to the grill can be brushed off into the fire.
• Do not clean the grill with soap or water, just scrub well with a wire brush (see equipment below). After cleaning, rub the flat plate with a little oil to season it and stop rust.
• If you have a gas or electric barbecue, clean in the same way. Special cleaners are also available from hardware stores.

Basic barbecue equipment
• Long handled tongs, so you don't burn yourself (don't leave them on or near the heat as they can get very hot).
• Bamboo or metal skewers. Metal can get very hot, so turn using a tea towel or tongs. Bamboo skewers are disposable and must be pre-soaked before use, to stop them burning.
• A sturdy wire brush for cleaning.

Food safety
• Barbecued food takes longer to cook: cook pork and poultry thoroughly and don't start cooking until the coals are ready.

the perfect picnic

Choose a spot that's easy to get to, preferably close to where you can park the car. It's all very well planning a romantic picnic at the top of a mountain, but don't forget that a picnic basket can get very heavy, very quickly!

Comfort
• If you have a car, take light, collapsible tables and chairs.
• Take plenty of rugs and cushions.
• Choose a shady place to spread your picnic blanket.
• Pack lanterns, torches and citronella tea-lights for evening.

Storage
• Safety and convenience are the most important elements.
• Use chill boxes. Pack the base with freezer blocks and put raw ingredients on the bottom and more delicate ones on top. This is also the best method for carrying ice cubes.
• Refrigerate precooked or prepared food until ready to pack.
• Remove marinated meat or fish from the refrigerator 1 hour before cooking and return to room temperature. It will cook more quickly, reducing the risk of undercooking and spoiling.
• Chill and store the food in the same container; plastic containers, zip lock bags and thermos flasks are all good. Plastic or glass bottles are good for drinks, dressings or syrups.
• Wrap sandwiches and rolls in baking parchment, then in foil. Store and transport cakes in their tins.
• Hardware and office supply stores sell aluminium storage tins. Cookware shops and Asian stores also sell stackable stainless steel lunch boxes – ideal for small snack dishes.

Transport
• Picnic baskets are romantic, but often impractical. When full, they're very heavy and hard for one person to carry. I prefer a two-handled basket to share the load.
• Use paper plates and plastic beakers – or glasses and plates wrapped individually in kitchen paper or cloth to avoid breakage.
• For adventurous picnics, pack non-perishable foods that can be eaten with your fingers. For easy transport, use a backpack.

index